❧ PROFILES OF GREAT ❧
BLACK AMERICANS

Jazz Stars

❧❧

Edited by Richard Rennert
Introduction by Coretta Scott King

⦀ A Chelsea House
⦀ Multibiography

Chelsea House Publishers
New York Philadelphia

On the cover: The Duke Ellington band performs at the Oriental
Theatre in Chicago in 1932.

Copyright © 1994 by Chelsea House Publishers, a division of
Main Line Book Co. All rights reserved. Printed and bound in the
United States of America.

First Printing

1 3 5 7 9 8 6 4 2

Library of Congress Cataloging-in-Publication Data

Jazz Stars/edited by Richard Rennert.
p. cm.—(Profiles of great Black Americans)
(A Chelsea House multibiography)
Includes bibliographical references and index.
Contents: Louis Armstrong—Count Basie—John Coltrane—
Duke Ellington—Ella Fitzgerald—Dizzy Gillespie—
Billie Holiday—Charlie Parker.
ISBN   0-7910-2059-2.
        0-7910-2060-6 (pbk.)
    1. Jazz musicians—United States—Biography—Juvenile
literature. 2. Afro-Americans—Biography—Juvenile literature.
[1. Musicians. 2. Jazz music. 3. Afro-Americans—Biography.]
I. Rennert, Richard. II. Series. III. Series: A Chelsea House
multibiography.
ML3929.J39 1993   93-16434
781.65'092'273—dc20   CIP
[B]   ·   AC MN

❧ CONTENTS ❧

❧ INTRODUCTION ❧
by Coretta Scott King

This book is about black Americans who served society through the excellence of their achievements. It forms a part of the rich history of black men and women in America—a history of stunning accomplishments in every field of human endeavor, from literature and art to science, industry, education, diplomacy, athletics, jurisprudence, even polar exploration.

Not all of the people in this history had the same ideals, but I think you will find something that all of them had in common. Like Martin Luther King, Jr., they all decided to become "drum majors" and serve humanity. In that principle—whether it was expressed in books, inventions, or song—they found something outside themselves to use as a goal and a guide. Something that showed them a way to serve others instead of only living for themselves.

Reading the stories of these courageous men and women not only helps us discover the principles that we will use to guide our own lives but also teaches us about our black heritage and about America itself. It is crucial for us to know the heroes and heroines of our history and to realize that the price we paid in our struggle for equality in America was dear. But we must also understand that we have gotten as far as we have partly because America's democratic system and ideals made it possible.

We are still struggling with racism and prejudice. But the great men and women in this series are a tribute to the spirit of our democratic ideals and the system in which they have flourished. And that makes their stories special and worth knowing.

LOUIS ARMSTRONG

One of the most acclaimed American musicians, the man who introduced the element of solo improvisation to jazz, thereby paving the way for its transformation from popular entertainment to serious art form, Louis Armstrong was born in 1899 in a house on Jane Alley in the Storyville section of New Orleans, Louisiana. His father, Willie Armstrong, who stoked a coal furnace for a turpentine manufacturer, deserted the family after Louis's birth, and he was raised by his mother, Mary Ann "Mayann" Miles Armstrong, and his paternal grandmother, Josephine Armstrong.

Nicknamed the Battlefield, the black section of Storyville was a notorious haunt of gamblers, hustlers, petty criminals, and prostitutes. Armstrong's home lacked running water, and he often had no shoes to wear. But for all Storyville's poverty, there was one thing there to inspire little Louis Armstrong—music. Storyville was the most musical section of a most musical city; its musicians played in dance halls, cafés, casinos, brothels, on street corners, and at funerals.

The music of Storyville was jazz, a uniquely American creation that combined many musical ideas. To the bright sounds of the marching band, jazz added driving African rhythms and the syncopations used by ragtime composers like Scott Joplin. Some of its melodies were witty and aggressive; others had a mournful quality derived from the spirituals of the black church. Jazz was exciting, funny, loud, and joyful and expressed many of the emotions that black people found necessary to mask in their day-to-day dealings with whites. When Louis Armstrong was growing up, the black musicians of Storyville were perfecting a unique New Orleans style of jazz that they called Dixieland.

As a boy, Armstrong sang in the streets for pennies from tourists, and his heroes were the great cornet players Buddy Bolden, Bunk Johnson, and Joseph "King" Oliver. At the age of 13, he was arrested for firing a pistol in the street and was sent to the Colored Waifs' Home, a reform school run by black social workers, where he joined the brass band and learned to play the cornet. After two years, he was released, and he returned to Storyville. By day he worked shoveling coal; by night he played with small bands in local saloons. He began to follow King Oliver around town, showing up wherever Oliver played with Kid Ory's Sunshine Orchestra. King Oliver encouraged Armstrong, and occasionally the eager young musician was even asked to sit in and play.

During World War I, military traffic through the port of New Orleans increased. With thousands of its sailors daily roaming the streets of the city, the navy insisted that the city close its houses of prostitution. As night spots shut down, the opportunities for musicians dwindled, and they began to leave for other cities. When Oliver left for Chicago, Armstrong replaced him as Kid Ory's cornetist. In 1918, he married Daisy Parker, a former prostitute, and began to play with Fate Marable's orchestra, which worked on the big paddle boats that ran up and down the Mississippi River.

It was aboard these elegant floating casinos and dance halls that Armstrong learned to read music. And although he was required to play formal arrangements of dance music, it was on the riverboats that Armstrong first revealed his genius for improvisation. In the middle of a live performance, during a cornet solo or while supporting other instruments, he would spontaneously compose new variations, and the melodies, harmonies, and rhythms always "fit" what the other players were doing.

In 1922, with his marriage rapidly failing, Armstrong left New Orleans for Chicago and a spot with King Oliver's Creole Jazz Band. For two years, Armstrong played with his mentor and idol's band, always in the great cornetist's shadow, but after his marriage to the group's piano player, Lil Hardin, in 1924, she encouraged him to strike out on his own. Armstrong took his wife's advice and lit out for New York to work for Fletcher Henderson's Black Swan Troubadours at the Roseland dance hall.

New Yorkers were hungry for good jazz. The city was then experiencing the glorious effects of the so-called Harlem Renaissance, and nowhere else in America were black writers, artists, and musicians making such an impact on culture. In such a heady atmosphere, Armstrong continued to grow artistically and to perfect his improvisational method, and he began to cut records, most notably five sides recorded in 1925 with Bessie Smith, the enormously popular "empress of the blues." But despite his success—"I went mad with the rest of the town," a colleague said about hearing Armstrong play for the first time—Armstrong soon grew restless with the Henderson group and returned to Chicago.

Over the next three years, Armstrong, as the head of a new band that he called Louis Armstrong and His Hot Five (soon expanded to the Hot Seven)—the other original members were clarinetist Johnny Dodds, trombonist Kid Ory, banjoist Johnny St. Cyr, drummer Baby Dodds, and pianist Lil Hardin—made more than 50 recordings that forever changed the course of American music. The group's first hit, "Heebie Jeebies," was followed in short course by electrifying new versions of "Muskrat Ramble," "St. James Infirmary," and the now legendary "West End Blues," which featured Earl "Fatha" Hines on piano. Armstrong's emotive tone on his instrument (he was now playing the trumpet rather than the cornet), his improvisational techniques, and his raspy "scat" singing, in which he replaced the lyrics of a song with nonsense syllables, made jazz musicians and listeners all over the country take notice. He was fast becoming a star.

In 1928, Prohibition came to Chicago, and as speakeasies and saloons shut down, musicians were thrown out of work. Armstrong returned to New York, playing at the Savoy Ballroom in Harlem and then working in the orchestra for the Broadway revue *Hot Chocolates*, composed by Thomas "Fats" Waller. Broadway gave Armstrong a taste of fame and fortune. He stopped performing with small jazz ensembles and put together larger bands that showcased his own playing. In 1932, he toured London and Paris, where American jazz was becoming popular. Onstage, he referred to himself as "Satchelmouth" because of his wide, trademark grin; a British journalist heard him wrong and coined the nickname "Satchmo," which soon caught on.

Though his personal life during this time was tumultuous (he would divorce Lil and marry twice more), and his business affairs were often in disarray (the artist was often the victim of unscrupulous promoters and managers), Armstrong was now entering the period of his greatest popularity. A crowd-pleasing showman as well as a profoundly serious artist, Armstrong by the end of the 1930s played regularly at the best jazz clubs in New York and Chicago, made appearances in Hollywood films, and reached millions of listeners with his recordings. During World War II, he toured the battlefields of Europe, entertaining American troops.

After the war, a new style of less melodic, more rhythmically and harmonically complex jazz called bebop captured the critical vanguard and the ears of younger listeners—"those cats play all the wrong notes," Armstrong complained of pioneer beboppers such as Charlie Parker, Dizzy Gillespie, and Thelonious Monk—but Armstrong, whose improvisations had paved the way for the even more ambitious forays of bebop's soloists, remained personally popular. With such masterful instrumentalists of his own generation as Earl Hines, clarinetist Barney Bigard, and trombonist Jack Teagarden, he put together a new small group, Louis Armstrong and the All Stars, with whom he toured incessantly, both in the United States and abroad.

Though critics argued that his best work was behind him, Armstrong achieved a new level of popular success in the late 1950s with his hit recordings of "Blueberry Hill" and "Mack the Knife." In 1964, he achieved the singular feat of knocking the Beatles from their number-one perch on the nation's pop chart with his vocal rendition of the title song from the Broadway smash *Hello, Dolly!*

While his fame remained undiminished, by the end of the 1960s Armstrong's health, compromised by his perennially grueling performance schedule, began to fail. In 1969, he spent three months in a New York hospital with heart and kidney problems. Persistent bronchitis made both singing and trumpet playing painful, and he began to spend an increasing amount of time with his wife, Lucille Wilson, in their Queens apartment. On July 6, 1971, at the age of 72, he died of kidney failure.

The world mourned his passing. One of the most popular musicians of his time as well as a serious artist and musical pioneer, Armstrong created an audience for jazz outside the black communities and beyond the borders of the United States. His influence remains immeasurable. "Nobody was bigger than Louis," Barney Bigard wrote about his friend—words that are as true today as ever.

COUNT BASIE

One of America's pre-eminent jazz pianists and bandleaders for more than 50 years, William Basie was born in Red Bank, New Jersey, on August 21, 1904. His father, Harvey Basie, was a groundskeeper on a nearby estate, and his mother, Lilly Ann, earned a little extra money for the family by taking in clothes for washing and ironing. The family was poor, but comfortable.

Both of Basie's parents played musical instruments, and they encouraged their son's interest in music at an early age. Basie started with the drums, but at the age of 15 he switched to the piano and began to play the ragtime tunes composers Scott Joplin and Tom Turpin had made popular in the 1890s.

In the days of silent films, movie theaters employed live piano players to accompany the action on-screen. Basie got his first break one night when the piano player at a local theater got sick and he was asked to fill in. He did so well that the theater manager offered him the chance to perform onstage with a band.

Seizing the opportunity, Basie and three friends formed a jazz quartet and were soon widely in demand as performers at dances, parties, and local clubs. He was quickly so successful as a professional musician that he dropped out of high school, a decision that he later said he regretted. After playing for a short time with Harry Richardson's Sunny Kings of Syncopation at the Hongkong Inn in Asbury Park, in 1924 he was lured to New York City by the flourishing music scene in the black community of Harlem.

Basie's skillful playing impressed a Harlem band-leader, and he got a job backing up a vocalist with the *Hippity Hop* traveling vaudeville show that kept him touring the country for over a year. Back in Harlem in 1925, he played regularly at famous night spots like Leroy's and the Rhythm Club, where after hours other local musicians would drop by to hold jam sessions and cutting contests in which they competed with each other to sharpen their chops. Under the influence of the stride piano style of James P. Johnson and the wild improvisations of Thomas "Fats" Waller, perhaps the two foremost jazz pianists of the day, Basie's playing became looser and more mellow.

Left stranded and broke in Kansas City in 1927 when the band with which he was touring broke up, Basie landed in a hospital for four months with a case of spinal meningitis. After his release, he tried to make ends meet by once again playing piano for silent films in a local movie house; to make his name known among local musicians, he circulated business cards on which he called himself the Count, imitating the noble nicknames of jazzmen like King Oliver and Duke Ellington.

In 1928, Basie went on tour with Walter Page and his Blue Devils, an outfit out of Oklahoma City that produced a smooth, synchronized, big-band sound using a strong rhythm section that would exert a great influence on Basie's style. In 1929, he returned to Kansas City's thriving jazz scene and began to play with the Bennie Moten Orchestra, with whom he toured the Southwest and performed on his first recordings. When Moten died tragically in 1935 as a result of a botched tonsillectomy, Basie formed his own band, the Barons of Rhythm, which performed regularly at Kansas City's Reno Club and soon attracted the favorable attention of record producer John Hammond.

As a result, in 1936 the Barons of Rhythm secured a recording contract. Basie now gave his group a new name—Count Basie and His Orchestra—and enlarged it from 9 to 15 musicians, including a rhythm section, four trumpets, and three trombones, a lineup that allowed him to begin creating the disciplined, velvety, big-band sound that would become the hall-mark of the Basie style.

Although the orchestra's first performances, at such venues as Chicago's Grand Terrace Ballroom and Roseland in New York City, were somewhat ragged and were not especially well received, the group soon jelled and began producing the smooth, tight, yet swinging sound that Basie desired. In 1937, Count Basie and His Orchestra opened at Harlem's prestigious Apollo Theater with its new vocalist, Billie Holiday, who stayed with the band for a year. Success at the Apollo opened doors, and soon the group was appearing all over the East Coast, in Baltimore, Philadelphia, and Washington, steadily building a national reputation.

In performance and on the more than 50 recordings that the orchestra made for Decca Records, which include such timeless American classics as "Pennies from Heaven," "Roseland Shuffle," "Jumpin' at the Woodside," and "One O'Clock Jump," Basie's piano did not dominate the band but laid out a simple melodic line that pulled the other instruments together and gave his soloists space to shine in. His embellishments and improvisations were gentle and supportive and served to highlight the contributions of such virtuoso instrumentalists and musicians as smooth trumpeter Buck Clayton, innovative saxophonists Lester Young and Herschel Evans, rhythm guitarist Freddie Green, and powerhouse vocalist Jimmy Rushing; most often he used the piano as a rhythm instrument to back up the more flamboyant forays of the reeds and horns. Basie's was a style that often caused him to be underappreciated as an instrumentalist, though seldom by fellow musicians. "Basie don't play nothing," said one such colleague, "but it sure sounds good."

By the end of 1937, jazz fans were lining up in the streets to hear the new Kansas City sound, and Basie was rapidly becoming as popular as the famed Duke Ellington and the leaders of other celebrated big bands. Engagements in New York City at Harlem's Savoy Ballroom and other venues were commercially and critically successful, and in January 1938, Basie and four members of his band were invited onstage for a jam session by Benny Goodman, the phenomenally popular clarinetist and "king of swing," at his legendary Carnegie Hall concert. In the 1940s, the Count Basie Orchestra toured the country several times and was featured in several Hollywood films. The decade was good to Basie personally as well as professionally; in 1942, he married Catherine Morgan, a vaudeville dancer. The couple would be parents to four children, three of them adopted.

By the late 1940s, the Count Basie Orchestra, like many other big bands, began to experience problems. The rationing of gasoline during World War II made touring more difficult. Old musicians left the group and new ones joined, eliminating the natural camaraderie that had contributed so much to the band's unique harmonious sound. Arrangements had to be written down and taught formally to the band members, causing much of the spontaneity and improvisational quality of the group's best music to be lost. The public's musical tastes were changing; the era of swing and the big bands was coming to an end.

In 1950, Basie broke up his orchestra. For the next two years, he toured with smaller bands of six to eight musicians. These new enterprises were popular and successful, but Basie missed the big-band sound. In 1952, he and saxophonist Marshall Royal formed a new Count Basie Orchestra. Most of the musicians were new, and the music itself was fresh and even more polished than the earlier arrangements. Basie explained the difference by saying that he had "put mink coats on the chords."

Basie's second band was enormously popular, and in 1954 it made the first of several European tours. Vocalist Joe Williams's rendition of "Every Day I Have the Blues" pushed it to the top of the charts in 1955, and there were performances and recording sessions with Duke Ellington, Sarah Vaughan, Ella Fitzgerald, Tony Bennett, Frank Sinatra, and Sammy Davis, Jr. By the 1960s, Basie was as popular as ever, and he was asked to perform at the inaugurations of presidents John F. Kennedy and Lyndon Johnson. In 1969, when American astronauts first set foot on the moon, the song they chose to broadcast back to earth was "Fly Me to the Moon," featuring Frank Sinatra and the Count Basie Orchestra.

Despite his advancing age, Basie continued to perform as often as possible, constantly touring the United States and in 1971 taking his band to the Far

East; the pace soon took its toll on his health. In 1976, he suffered a heart attack; though he returned to performing after a six-month layoff, by 1980 he was so crippled by arthritis that he used a motor scooter to reach the stage.

Count Basie died of cancer on April 26, 1984, soon after completing his autobiography, *Good Morning Blues*. At his funeral at the Abyssinian Baptist Church in Harlem, Joe Williams sang a spiritual composed by Duke Ellington, Basie's only real rival, in terms of influence and historical importance, as a leader of big bands. His beloved orchestra lived on; under Thad Jones and Frank Foster it has continued to thrill listeners with its jazz mastery, reminding them of what Basie and many others always believed about his band—"that they were the best on the planet earth."

JOHN COLTRANE

A saxophonist whose legend grows with every passing year, John Coltrane was born in Hamlet, North Carolina, on September 23, 1926, into a proud and well-respected family. His maternal grandfather, William Blair, was a prominent preacher; his father, John, Sr., was a skilled tailor and a gifted amateur musician. John, Jr., grew into a strong, athletic young man who had a gentle and thoughtful nature. At the age of 12 he joined a community band in the town of High Point, where the family had moved shortly after his birth, and took up the clarinet. As he learned more about music, he became interested in the saxophone and hoped to someday follow in the footsteps of the jazz greats Lester Young and Johnny Hodges.

The Coltrane family began to fragment when John was in his teens. His grandfather and father both died within a short space of time, a double loss that appears to have had long-lasting effects on John. After the outbreak of World War II in 1941, John's mother, Alice, moved north to Philadelphia in order to take advantage of the high wages being offered for war-related factory work. In 1943, when he graduated from high school, John joined his mother. Alice Coltrane supported her son's decision to pursue a musical career instead of attending college. During the day he worked in a sugar refinery, and at night he studied saxophone at the Ornstein School of Music. In 1945, he was drafted and spent the final year of the war in Hawaii, playing clarinet in a U.S. Navy band.

When he returned from the service in 1946, Coltrane resumed his music studies. He was living with his mother and his aunt, and both women encouraged him to devote all his time to music. Typically, he practiced late into the night, diligently going over the finger positions on his horn without blowing so as to avoid disturbing the neighbors. He also began to play in a number of rhythm-and-blues bands, and at this time he switched from the alto saxophone to the deeper-toned tenor saxophone, on which he was eventually to make his reputation.

During the late 1940s and early 1950s, Coltrane continued to develop his musical skills, studying and practicing relentlessly in the conviction that he was destined to become a great musician. He played and recorded with a number of leading musicians, including Dizzy Gillespie and Johnny Hodges, one of his boyhood idols. In 1955, his life changed in two significant ways: he married Juanita Grubbs, known as Naima, and he joined musical forces with the young trumpeter Miles Davis.

Davis, who was the same age as Coltrane, was regarded as the most exciting figure in jazz, the heir apparent to the brilliant saxophonist Charlie Parker, who had recently died. Coltrane was introduced to Davis by the drummer "Philly" Joe Jones; when Davis put together a group consisting of Jones, pianist Red Garland, and bassist Paul Chambers, he invited Coltrane to join. Now considered one of the great ensembles in the history of jazz, the group made its first recording, *The New Miles Davis Quintet*, in 1956, and followed up with several more. Coltrane did solid work on these recordings, but some critics felt that he was not at the same level as the other players.

Coltrane received a great deal of notice by working with Davis, but his mind was not always on his music. Always quiet and sensitive, he now became moody and withdrawn, and he was deeply involved with both heroin and alcohol. Davis, an intense and strong-willed individual, came to the conclusion that Coltrane was unreliable and asked him to leave the group in 1957, replacing him with another gifted saxophonist, Sonny Rollins.

After Coltrane's break with Davis, his family feared that he was on the verge of a mental and physical collapse, and they considered putting him into the hospital. Fortunately, Coltrane woke up one morning and announced that he was giving up drugs, liquor, and tobacco. For the better part of a week he remained in his room, consuming nothing but water. He emerged a changed man, and although he was known to smoke in later years, he never again touched drugs or alcohol.

Shortly after his recovery, Coltrane was invited to play with the pianist Thelonious Monk. Free of his emotional problems, he was able to absorb a great deal of musical knowledge from Monk, who was both a brilliant innovator and a prolific composer. At this time, Coltrane perfected his technique on the saxophone. Whereas most jazz musicians were able to improvise two or three related chords in place of the original chords in a song, Coltrane now found that he was able to insert *four*. In order to do this, he had to play as many as 1,000 notes a minute, a tremendous feat attainable only through years of practice. This technical mastery, in combination with his profound grasp of music theory, enabled Coltrane to create the cascades of sound that distinguished his breathtakingly dynamic and poetic solos.

After his stint with Monk, Coltrane rejoined the Miles Davis group, which was now a sextet, and played brilliantly on a number of acclaimed recordings, including *Kind of Blue*, regarded by many jazz fans as the finest jazz album ever made. In 1960, the group embarked on a highly successful European tour; at a March 22 concert in Stockholm, Sweden, Coltrane's playing reached heights achieved by few musicians in any field. When he returned to the United States, he knew that he was ready to go out on his own.

In 1960, Coltrane assembled a quartet that included pianist McCoy Tyner, drummer Elvin Jones, and bassist Steve Davis (later supplanted by Jimmy Garrison). Late in the year, the group released its first recording, *My Favorite Things*. Coltrane's work on the title track represents yet another musical experiment. Here he plays soprano saxophone and delves into a technique known as polytonality, common in 20th-century classical music but unusual in jazz. For all its novelty, the result was also appealing to the public: *My Favorite Things* enjoyed substantial sales and made Coltrane a major force in the jazz world.

Coltrane followed up his success with a series of now-classic albums, including *Crescent, Impressions, Meditations*, and *A Love Supreme*. *A Love Supreme*, released in 1964, had a special appeal for the young generation of Americans that was drawing its main inspiration from rock 'n' roll and taking a keen interest in non-Western cultures. In addition to its musical

excitement, the album celebrated the spiritual principles of the Eastern religions, which Coltrane had
found increasingly attractive since his personal resur-
rection in 1957. *A Love Supreme* sold more than
250,000 copies and made Coltrane a genuine cult
figure, a musician whom many fans considered to be
endowed with mystical powers.

While he was earning widespread adulation,
Coltrane was enjoying a happy family life. His marriage to Naima had ended, but in 1963 he met the
pianist Alice McLeod, whom he married two years
later. When he was not playing, Coltrane spent most
of his time in his spacious Long Island home, enjoying
his children, practicing, gardening, and reading books
on spiritual subjects.

However, Coltrane was not content to bask in his
celebrity, nor did his commercial success cause him to
grow artistically complacent. Even while making his
most successful recordings, he had been experimenting with the style known as free jazz, pioneered by
fellow saxophonist Ornette Coleman. In free jazz,
musicians ignored the traditional chord changes and
punctuated their solos with seemingly disconnected
notes—in the case of saxophonists, startling shrieks
and growls that disconcerted some listeners while
intriguing others. Coltrane released his first free-jazz
album, *Ascension*, in 1965 and continued to work in
that style for the next two years.

By 1967, no one was sure what direction Coltrane's
music would take. He was known to be in seclusion,
preparing material that he felt was not yet ready for

public exposure. Before long, it also became apparent that Coltrane was seriously ill. He had for some time been suffering from pain in his abdomen, and the doctors eventually diagnosed his ailment as cancer of the liver. Coltrane remained at home as long as possible, but on July 16 he checked himself into the hospital. He died the following day, two months short of his 41st birthday. Speaking to an interviewer a few years earlier, he expressed a thought that poignantly sums up his musical legacy: "I think the main thing a musician would like to do is to give a picture to the listener of the many wonderful things he knows of and senses in the universe." Succeeding generations of listeners—and musicians—are still reaping fresh insights from John Coltrane's vision.

DUKE ELLINGTON

Pianist, bandleader, and America's most prolific and accomplished jazz composer, Edward Kennedy Ellington was born on April 29, 1899, in Washington, D.C. His father, James Edward Ellington, was a charming and dashing man who worked as a butler, a caterer, and later as a blueprint maker for the navy. His mother, Daisy Ellington, pampered young Edward, whom she always referred to as her "jewel." Both parents loved music and played the piano, but as a youngster their only son preferred baseball to music lessons. That ended one day when Daisy saw her jewel accidentally get hit on the head with a baseball bat. She decided then and there that piano lessons were a much safer activity for her beloved boy.

Ellington's lessons—the only formal music instruction he would ever receive—lasted only a short time. At first, he was still more interested in playing baseball, but after hearing a young pianist named Harvey Brooks play, he decided that he, too, would master the instrument, and he gave up sports for music. "I learned that when you were playing the piano there was always a pretty girl standing down near the bass clef end of the piano. I ain't been no athlete since," he once said in explaining his decision.

Ellington began to practice on his own, and he was soon playing his own compositions at friends' parties. Because he had grown into a handsome, snappily dressed, suave young man, a friend nicknamed him Duke. He attached himself to a local piano player, Oliver "Doc" Perry, and learned the tricks of all the popular styles—ragtime, stride, and jazz. A talented painter as well, Ellington made a fateful decision after graduating high school and turned down a scholarship to Pratt Institute in Brooklyn, New York, in order to continue playing music. He spent several years working for Louis Thomas, a nightclub owner who booked him to play at dances and dinner parties, and in 1918, he married Edna Thompson, his high school sweetheart. Soon he began to organize and book bands on his own.

In 1919, Ellington went to hear the greatest of the stride pianists, James P. Johnson, perform at Convention Hall in Washington. Eager to see if the local favorite could outplay the celebrated Johnson, friends pushed Ellington onstage for a "cutting contest." Impressed with Ellington's playing, Johnson became a lifelong friend and teacher. "What I absorbed on that occasion," Ellington said, "might have constituted a whole semester in a conservatory."

By the early 1920s, Ellington had assembled a superior group of musicians dedicated to good music and to Ellington himself, but Washington was not a big music town, and opportunities were limited. In 1923, Ellington, along with saxophonist Otto "Toby" Hardwick and drummer Sonny Greer, went to New York to break into the music scene in the predominantly black community of Harlem, which was then enjoying its famed Harlem Renaissance—an explosion of new ideas and talent in the fields of music, literature, and the other arts. "We were awed by the never-ending roll of great talents there," Ellington said. "Harlem to our minds did indeed have the world's most glamorous atmosphere. We had to go there." They formed Duke Ellington and the Washingtonians and began to draw big crowds at Barron's Exclusive Club. After moving his group to the Kentucky Club, Ellington met Irving Mills, a struggling music publisher who became his business partner for the next 15 years. Mills insisted that Ellington retain the rights to his songs and compositions and that he record only his own works so that he would earn more of the income from a hit record. Ellington and Mills would make each other rich, and income from Ellington's more than 2,000 original jazz compositions would support his band members when times were hard.

By the mid-1920s, the Washingtonians had added Bubber Miley on trumpet, Barney Bigard on clarinet, Joe "Tricky Sam" Nanton on trombone, and Harry Carney on baritone sax. They quickly evolved from a dance band into a jazz band, perfecting a unique, deeply rhythmic kind of jazz known as jungle style. Their big break came in 1927, when Mills booked the Washingtonians into Harlem's most famous night spot, the Cotton Club. Under the new name of Duke Ellington and His Orchestra, the band was a smash. They were soon making live radio broadcasts from the Cotton Club and becoming well known across the country for such hit songs as "Creole Love Call," "East St. Louis Toodle-oo," and "Black and Tan Fantasy."

By the early 1930s, Ellington was a nationally known bandleader and symbol of the Harlem Renaissance, and the "Ellington sound" was recognized by jazz fans all across the country. But Ellington's private ambition was to compose innovative new jazz pieces as serious instrumental music. He abandoned the "jungle style" and began to create more sophisticated compositions with complex, symphonylike orchestrations. His 1930 hits "Mood Indigo" and "Creole

Rhapsody" demonstrated the change, but the orchestra still sustained itself with Ellington's more traditional songs at clubs and dance halls. Trombonist Lawrence Brown, trumpet player Cootie Williams, bass player Jimmy Blanton, saxophonists Johnny Hodges and Ben Webster, and vocalist Ivie Anderson joined the orchestra, and with its expanded size it began to take on a big-band sound and some of the elements of the new style of swing, which used the piano, guitar, bass, and drums as a special rhythm section to hold the beat for dancers. Ellington's hits of this period included "In a Sentimental Mood," "Solitude," and "Echoes of Harlem."

In collaboration with composer and arranger Billy Strayhorn, Ellington enjoyed the most creative period of his career in the early 1940s. He scored hits with "Sophisticated Lady," "I Got It Bad (And That Ain't Good)," and "Concerto for Cootie." In 1941, Ellington established his own music publishing company—a most unusual achievement for a black artist in those days—and his orchestra recorded what would become its signature tune, "Take the A Train," as well as his music for the Hollywood revue *Jump for Joy*, a celebration of black life in America.

On January 23, 1943, Duke Ellington and His Orchestra became the first black jazz band to perform at New York's Carnegie Hall, an appearance that became an annual event through the early 1950s. By the late 1940s, however, big-band jazz seemed to be dying. A new generation of musicians—among them Dizzy Gillespie, Thelonious Monk, and Charlie

Parker—was inventing a sophisticated new kind of jazz, called bebop, that was intended more for listening than dancing. The crowds the big bands counted on turned to the music of the popular crooners.

Ellington managed to keep his orchestra together, but several key musicians left, including Sonny Greer and Lawrence Brown, and the band's playing during the early 1950s seemed uninspired. But in 1956, Ellington signed a contract with Columbia Records and rerecorded some earlier pieces with new arrangements for a band that now included a younger group of musicians. The rejuvenated sound of the Ellington orchestra caught on. In the same year, Ellington performed to great acclaim at the Newport Jazz Festival, introducing his music to a younger audience, and he was soon as popular as ever. In 1958 and 1959, the orchestra toured Europe. There were bold new compositions as well, like *A Drum Is a Woman* and *Such Sweet Thunder*, and recording sessions with avant-garde artists such as John Coltrane. In 1963, the orchestra toured Africa, Asia, and the Middle East at the request of the State Department. In 1965, Ellington wrote the Sacred Concerts to celebrate the opening of Grace Cathedral in San Francisco; in 1968, he won two Grammy Awards from the National Academy of Recording Arts and Sciences. In the 1970s, there were more world tours and exciting new compositions like New Orleans Suite, *Afro-Eurasian Eclipse*, and *The River*.

In 1973, Ellington discovered that he had terminal cancer. He finished his autobiography, *Music Is My*

Mistress, and died on May 24, 1974, at the age of 75. His son, Mercer Ellington, took over the orchestra and has kept it alive to the present day. Ellington still has millions of fans, his greatest recordings are re-issued yearly, and each new generation of jazz musicians rediscovers his music. A giant among jazz personalities, a brilliant pianist, creator, and leader of the greatest American jazz band, today more than ever Ellington stands alone as the foremost jazz composer.

ELLA FITZGERALD

Known to her fans as the First Lady of Song, Ella Fitzgerald was born in Newport News, Virginia, on April 25, 1918. Her father died shortly after she was born, and her mother soon took her to live in Yonkers, New York. Though times were always hard, Tempie Fitzgerald, who loved music, did everything she could to encourage her daughter's budding talent.

Ella studied music as a child, but her first love was dancing rather than singing. In 1934, at the age of 16, she entered a talent contest at the Harlem Opera House, where the audiences were known to have little patience for bumblers. When it was her turn to go onstage and dance, the teenager was almost paralyzed by fear and stood trembling before the audience. Desperate to avoid being hooted off the stage, she began to sing "Judy," a song she had often heard on the radio—by the time she was done, the audience was cheering, and she was clutching a $25 prize.

Fitzgerald now knew that she had the ability to succeed as a singer, but work was hard to find in the midst of the economic depression gripping the country. To make matters worse, her mother died, leaving her in the care of an aunt. Fitzgerald's big break came when she was introduced to Chick Webb, the diminutive drummer who led one of the leading swing bands of the day. Webb was impressed by Fitzgerald's voice, and despite her youth and inexperience he hired her as a singer. Webb and his wife, Sallye, also became Fitzgerald's legal guardians, taking her into their home and treating her like a daughter.

Fitzgerald played many dates with Webb's band at the Savoy Ballroom in Harlem and made her first record, "Love and Kisses," in 1935. She was now being taken very seriously by jazz fans, who marveled at her vocal range and her seemingly effortless mastery of pitch and harmony: by 1937, she had won the *Down Beat* magazine poll as Best Female Vocalist of the year.

The record that made Fitzgerald nationally known at the age of 20 was "A-Tisket, A-Tasket," a swinging rendition of the old nursery rhyme that Fitzgerald worked out with one of Webb's music arrangers, Al Feldman. The toe-tapping disk became a smash hit in 1938, topping the charts for 17 weeks in a row. Fitzgerald and Webb followed up on the record's success with appearances at posh New York hotels and Broadway theaters, in some cases breaking racial barriers by being the first black musicians to perform in these venues. In 1939, however, the warmhearted and talented Webb died of pneumonia, leaving Fitzgerald on her own once again.

Unsure of her future, Fitzgerald was surprised and gratified when Webb's former manager, Moe Gale, insisted that the band be kept together and renamed Ella Fitzgerald and Her Orchestra. Though a number of the band members actually ran the show, the change of title was a tribute to Fitzgerald's stature in the music world. For two years the band traveled throughout the United States, playing to wildly enthusiastic audiences.

When the United States entered World War II in December 1941, the big-band era effectively died; many musicians joined the armed forces, and gasoline rationing made large-scale touring impossible. The demise of the big band brought vocalists into the limelight; though recording activity was suspended due to a lengthy musicians' strike, Fitzgerald traveled to Hollywood to make a movie and appeared with the popular quartet known as the Four Keys. When recording resumed, she found herself much in demand, but she was asked to perform the sentimental ballads in vogue during the war years, when so many couples were separated.

Fitzgerald's talent could not be so confined for long. Yearning to return to jazz, she found herself drawn to bebop, the new style of playing that featured quicker tempos and sudden shifts of rhythm and harmony. Joining the band led by Dizzy Gillespie, the trumpet player who was one of bebop's pioneers, Fitzgerald worked out the vocal equivalent of bop instrumentals by singing scat, a technique originally developed by the early jazz titan Louis Armstrong. Instead of singing the words to a song, Fitzgerald would use her voice like a trumpet or a saxophone, improvising a rapid string of syllables that would propel the music in surprising and exhilarating directions. In 1947, she recorded two scat songs, "Oh Lady Be Good" and "How High the Moon." Both records became hits, establishing a style that was ever after identified with Fitzgerald.

Nineteen forty-eight was a pivotal year for Fitzgerald. First she married bassist Ray Brown and settled down with him in Queens, New York. In the same year, she met Norman Granz, a young music promoter who was eager to be a part of her career. Because Granz was known both for his commitment to jazz and for his willingness to champion the rights of black musicians, Fitzgerald agreed to work with him.

Granz immediately booked Fitzgerald into his "Jazz at the Philharmonic" tour, which had begun in 1944 and included such jazz greats as Lester Young, Oscar Peterson, and Roy Eldridge. Fitzgerald loved the tour and took all the hardships of the traveling musician's life in stride—even when Granz's insistence on integrated audiences caused trouble in the segregated South. "Jazz at the Philharmonic" took Fitzgerald all over the United States, as well as to Europe and Japan, where she gained legions of new fans. As Granz watched her perform year after year, he became convinced that despite her repeated triumphs, Fitzgerald had not yet tapped her full potential. He was so convinced of this that he offered to be her manager for a year without receiving any pay. Fitzgerald decided to give him a chance.

When Granz became Fitzgerald's manager in 1954, the first thing he did was to negotiate a release from her recording contract with Decca Records. He then signed her up with Verve, his own label. The extended-play record was just coming into vogue at this time, and Granz convinced Fitzgerald to record an album of Broadway show tunes, a project never before tackled by a singer with her gifts. *The Cole Porter Songbook*, released in 1956, was a revelation to listeners, who snapped up more than 100,000 copies, a phenomenal figure for that time. Within the next few years, Fitzgerald recorded albums dedicated to all the great American songwriters: Jerome Kern, George and Ira Gershwin, Harold Arlen, Irving Berlin, Duke Ellington, Johnny Mercer, and Rogers and

Hart. Each one a classic in its own right, together these albums endure as a treasury of American popular music. True to Granz's expectations, they earned Fitgerald healthy royalties and made her a household name throughout the country.

During the 1960s, when rock 'n' roll replaced more traditional forms of music at the top of the charts, Fitzgerald began to work less than she had in previous years. She had resettled in Beverly Hills, California, and was content to spend more time at home with her young son, Ray, Jr. (Her marriage to Ray Brown had ended after five years.) In the 1970s, interest in jazz began to revive, and Fitzgerald was in great demand for concert dates and even television commercials. As the extent of her achievements became more and more evident, a number of leading universities and colleges, including Yale and Dartmouth, awarded her honorary degrees in music, and the University of Maryland named its performing arts center after her.

Fitzgerald's health began to deteriorate during the 1980s, and at one point she had to undergo open-heart surgery. But she has bounced back from every illness, and her annual appearances at the JVC Jazz Festival in New York City are anticipated by music fans as one of the highlights of the year. In 1993, the Schomburg Center for Research in Black Culture held a celebration at New York's Carnegie Hall in honor of Fitzgerald's 75th birthday. Luminaries from all the arts gathered to express their love and admiration for Fitzgerald and to commemorate one more milestone in a life filled with breathtaking accomplishments. To name just a few, Fitzgerald had been named the top female jazz singer for 18 years in a row in the *Down Beat* poll and for 13 years in a row in the *Playboy* poll; she had won more Grammy awards than any other female vocalist in history; she had been previously feted at Washington's Kennedy Center, an honor accorded only to legendary entertainers; she had received the Whitney Young Award from the National Urban League for her contributions to African-American life; and the president of the United States had presented her with the National Medal of the Arts. Summing up the spirit and dedication that brought her to these heights, Fitzgerald once declared, "The only thing better than singing is more singing."

DIZZY GILLESPIE

One of the greatest innovators in American musical history, John Birks Gillespie was born on October 21, 1917, in Cheraw, South Carolina. His father worked as a bricklayer to support his nine children, but in his spare time he played piano for a number of bands that traveled up and down the eastern seaboard. Growing up in a home filled with musical instruments, young John fell in love with music and dreamed of someday playing in a big-time band.

When John was 10 years old his father died, and the youngster's grief drove him to become a troublemaker who was constantly in fights at school. Fortunately for him, a dedicated music teacher named Alice Wilson took an interest in him and convinced him to take up the trombone. By the time he was 12, John was playing both the trombone and the trumpet and was working hard to make himself a truly skilled musician.

When Gillespie was 16, his mother moved the family north to Philadelphia in search of a better life. Gillespie soon found that he could earn money with his trumpet and decided to make music his career. Like most jazz musicians during the 1930s, Gillespie began his career playing swing music in big bands. His idol was the leading jazz trumpeter of the day, Roy Eldridge. Eldridge was admired for his ability to play at great speed, with unexpected swoops and turns, and Gillespie began to copy his style. He did it so well that radio broadcast listeners often could not tell which of the two trumpeters they were hearing.

Because of his ability to play like Eldridge, Gillespie landed a job in Teddy Hill's band, which played regularly at the Savoy Ballroom in New York City's Harlem. During this time, he developed a flair for outlandish outfits that often featured a baggy suit, loud tie, wide-brimmed hat or beret, and a long cigarette holder. He loved to wisecrack and play practical jokes on his fellow musicians; during shows he would often put his feet up on the music stand and perform other high-spirited pranks. Legend has it that one of his fellow band members began to call him Dizzy, and the name stuck for the rest of his life.

Clowning aside, Dizzy Gillespie could play. By the late 1930s, he was being included in recording sessions with some of the finest musicians in jazz, including Coleman Hawkins, Lionel Hampton, and Ben Webster.

When Gillespie joined Cab Calloway's band in 1939, he came into contact with musicians who were experimenting with new styles. The most important of them was the saxophonist Charlie Parker, whom Gillespie met in Kansas City while on tour with the Calloway band. Parker, Gillespie, and other musicians, such as pianist Thelonious Monk and drummer Kenny Clarke, would often get together and improvise music that was faster, more inventive, and more complex than the swing music played by the big bands.

The turning point in Gillespie's career came when he lost his regular job after a fight with Calloway. Gillespie now found that he could make a living on his own. He soon began to play and record with the leading lights in the world of jazz. By 1945, when he and Charlie Parker had completed such now-classic recordings as "Salt Peanuts," "Ko Ko," "Billie's Bounce," and "Woody 'n' You," he was at the forefront of the new jazz movement known as bebop, which was to remain the dominant influence on jazz for years to come.

Gillespie always gave Parker full credit as the co-inventor of bebop, but Parker was an unruly genius who often missed performances and recording dates, making it necessary for Gillespie to provide the actual leadership and stabilizing force. It was Gillespie who dealt with the record producers and club owners, making sure that all the business arrangements were scrupulously carried out. Unlike Parker and many other jazz musicians, Gillespie stayed away from drugs and alcohol and was careful with his money. He gave much of the credit for his levelheadedness to his wife, Lorraine, a former dancer, whom he married in 1940 and lived with happily for the rest of his life.

In 1946, Gillespie created the Dizzy Gillespie Orchestra and once again changed the history of jazz. He recruited two leading Cuban musicians, trumpeter Mario Bauza and drummer Chano Pozo, who brought conga and bongo drums into jazz for the first time. From this mix of black American bebop and Latin rhythms came a new music known as Afro-Cuban jazz. The numbers recorded by Gillespie's band—most notably "Manteca" and "Cubana Be, Cubana Bop"—exerted a lasting influence on both traditional jazz and Latin music.

The hallmark of bebop was the small combo, and Gillespie's greatest contribution in the eyes of many jazz fans was the remarkable quintet he formed in 1946 with Parker, pianist Bud Powell, drummer Max

Roach, and bassist Ray Brown. The quartet had an often stormy career, but in 1953 its members were reunited (with Charles Mingus sitting in on bass) for a concert at Massey Hall in Toronto, Canada. Playing before a wildly enthusiastic audience, Gillespie and his group turned in a sizzling performance that has since been hailed as "the greatest jazz concert ever."

By this time, Gillespie was not only a trumpeter without peer but also one of the leading figures in American entertainment. Like his fellow jazz great Louis Armstrong, he was beloved by the public as much for his exuberant personality as for his musical ability. Gillespie reveled in his role as a master showman. When someone accidentally bent his trumpet, he decided that he liked it better that way and had all his trumpets made in the same pattern from then on. The image of Gillespie blowing his horn, with his cheeks puffed out and the bell of his trumpet sticking up at a wild and jaunty angle, became one of the most distinctive sights in show business.

In 1956, Gillespie brought jazz to an international audience when the U.S. State Department provided him with the funds to conduct a world tour as a musical goodwill ambassador. Gillespie was the first bandleader asked to undertake such a mission. He put together a group of musicians that represented a racial, ethnic, and religious cross section of the United States and delighted foreign audiences with classic music making and high spirits. (In the course of the tour he was photographed riding camels, charming snakes with his trumpet, and wearing the native costumes of various countries.) During this stage of his career, he also served on the faculty of the Lenox School of Jazz in Massachusetts and made brilliant recordings with such jazz greats as Stan Getz and Sonny Rollins.

Unlike so many musicians of his generation, who either burned out at an early age or fell into neglect when styles changed, Gillespie never lost his verve or his public appeal. Throughout the 1960s and 1970s, he led a variety of big bands and small ensembles, which he took on extended tours. He also revived his recording career, and his new recordings won Grammy awards in 1975 and 1980.

During the 1980s, Gillespie assumed the role of an elder statesman in the jazz world, appearing as a guest artist with a variety of bands. His energy was undiminished: in 1989, at the age of 72, he gave 300 performances in 27 different countries. His stature was such that 14 universities awarded him honorary degrees; the French government decorated him with the Legion of Honor; and his own nation honored him with the National Medal of the Arts.

In the fall of 1992, the Blue Note in New York City engaged Gillespie for a monthlong appearance in honor of his 75th birthday. During the month, the greats of the jazz world joined Gillespie on the bandstand, paying tribute to him as a man and an artist, most of them unaware that he was afflicted with cancer of the pancreas. On January 6, 1993, Dizzy Gillespie died in Englewood, New Jersey, leaving behind a creative legacy seldom equaled by any American artist.

BILLIE HOLIDAY

$\mathbf{H}$ailed by critics as the greatest jazz singer who ever lived, Billie Holiday was born Eleanora Fagan in Baltimore, Maryland, on April 7, 1915. Her parents married after she was born and divorced when she was very young. Her father, Clarence Holiday, a traveling musician, soon disappeared from her life. When Eleanora's mother, Sadie Fagan, went north to work as a maid, Eleanora was left in the care of a cousin who often mistreated her. At the age of six, Eleanora went to work, scrubbing the steps of houses and doing chores in a brothel; there she heard the records of such early jazz greats as Louis Armstrong and Bessie Smith, and she forgot her troubles for a while by singing along with the music. She also began to call herself Billie after Billie Dove, a popular actress of the day.

When Billie was 10, a grown man tried to rape her; he was sent to jail, but the judge also ordered that Billie be confined in a reform school for her own protection. She endured two dreadful years in the institution before her mother managed to get her released. She then headed north to join her mother in Harlem, New York City's most important black neighborhood.

Life proved to be just as difficult in New York. Billie's mother worked long hours and had little time to look after her; by the time she was 13, Billie was working as a prostitute. After being arrested, she decided to find another way to survive, but with the arrival of the Great Depression in 1930, jobs became scarce. Before long, Billie and her mother had no money for their rent and were faced with eviction; searching desperately for some way to earn money, Billie entered a basement club named Pod's and Jerry's and asked for work as a dancer. The owner quickly saw that she was not a skilled dancer and was about to send her away. But the club's pianist felt sorry for her and gave her the chance to sing a popular song of the day, "Trav'lin' All Alone." As she sang, a hush fell over the crowded club, and some of the customers began to weep; when she was done, people threw money at her feet. Her career was launched.

Holiday was fortunate enough to arrive on the scene when jazz was taking hold of Harlem, and there were ample opportunities to perform in clubs and theaters. In these forums Holiday developed her unique singing style, improvising variations on familiar songs just as the leading jazz instrumentalists did. In 1933, Holiday came to the attention of the influential critic and producer John Hammond, who wrote about her in magazines and arranged for her first recording date.

Holiday's first real breakthrough occurred in 1935, when she had a successful engagement at Harlem's prestigious Apollo Theater. At this time, she also began to record in earnest, doing several sessions for the Brunswick label along with such star performers as pianist Teddy Wilson, clarinetist Benny Goodman, and saxophonist Ben Webster. The records established Holiday's reputation in the music world. She was soon able to buy a restaurant for her mother, and the two of them lived comfortably in an apartment upstairs.

Holiday also tried her hand at touring with the popular bands led by Count Basie and Artie Shaw, but she could not adjust to life on the road. Conditions were especially hard in the segregated South, where black musicians were barred from the better hotels and restaurants. Holiday soon decided that she was better off taking her chances in New York. She was now in demand as a recording artist; between 1936 and 1942, when a musicians' strike called a halt to recording, Holiday made a steady stream of disks for the Commodore label. As in her first recordings, she was backed by all the best players in jazz and was captured at the height of her form. The Commodore sides, wrote a later jazz historian, "constitute one of the major bodies of work in jazz."

In 1938, Holiday found the perfect showcase for her talents at Café Society, an integrated nightclub opened in Greenwich Village by Barney Josephson. In a nine-month engagement at the new club, Holiday became a full-fledged star. Combining her sophisticated vocal technique with raw emotional honesty, she made everything she sang—even the most shopworn standards—sound brand-new to her listeners. It was at Café Society that she first performed "Strange Fruit," a haunting, somber protest against the lynching of blacks in the South. When Holiday recorded the controversial song in 1939, she gained recognition not only as a singer but as a public figure.

During the 1940s, Holiday, now known to her fans simply as Lady Day, reached the peak of her popularity. She found steady work in the clubs sprouting up along West 52nd Street: the Onyx, the Spotlite, Kelly's Stable, and the Famous Door were among the night spots that signed her to sing before packed houses, paying her as much as $1,000 a week. At this time, Holiday began wearing a white gardenia in her hair, an elegant touch that soon became her trademark.

She also made two of her best-known recordings, "Gloomy Sunday" and "God Bless the Child."

Sadly, fame did not erase the memories of Holiday's painful childhood or ensure her a happy personal life. She had often been unfortunate in her choice of men, and this pattern continued when she married Jimmy Monroe in 1941. Monroe was an opium smoker, and Holiday soon shared his addiction to the potent narcotic. When the marriage began to come apart after little more than a year, Holiday turned to heroin. Before long, her drug habit was consuming half her earnings. "I was making a thousand a week," she later said, "but I had as much freedom as a field hand in Virginia a hundred years before."

For a time, Holiday's career continued to soar. She was voted Best Vocalist in an *Esquire* magazine poll in 1943 and two years later made her first concert appearance at New York's Town Hall. But she continued to use heroin, and the death of her mother in 1945 deprived her of the one person she could rely on for understanding and encouragement. More and more, she showed up late for performances or missed them altogether; she began to wear long white gloves onstage to hide the needle marks on her arms.

In May 1947, Holiday was arrested by federal narcotics agents on a drug possession charge. She threw herself on the mercy of the court, hoping that the judge would send her to a clinic for treatment. Instead, she was sentenced to a federal prison in West Virginia, where she underwent a harrowing drug withdrawal and endured nine and a half months of isolation and misery.

Those who knew Holiday well believed that she never recovered from the pain of her imprisonment. However, barely two weeks after her release, she enjoyed one of her greatest triumphs. Knowing how much her fans had missed her, Holiday's agent, Joe Glaser, booked her into New York's legendary Carnegie Hall. On March 27, 1948, a standing-room-only audience gave Holiday a tumultuous welcome. Her talents undiminished by her prison ordeal, she rewarded her cheering fans with one of her most brilliant performances.

Unfortunately, the concert did not completely revive Holiday's fortunes. Because of her prison record, she could not get a permit to sing in clubs; she earned a living during the 1950s with theater performances, but she eventually began using heroin again. Still she fought on, making a series of recordings for the Verve label and enjoying a highly successful 1954 tour of Europe.

In 1956, following another arrest, Holiday kicked her drug habit again. But she began to drink heavily, and her stage appearances were sometimes marred by drunkenness. Theater managers became wary of dealing with her, and audiences often came to see her out of curiosity, wondering if she would make it through her set. Once surrounded by admirers and hangers-on, Holiday now spent most of her time alone in a small apartment on Manhattan's West Side, drinking and watching television. In the spring of 1959, beset by heart and liver ailments, she finally collapsed. With hospital care her condition improved temporarily, but on July 17, Billie Holiday died at the age of 44. Thousands of fans attended her funeral, knowing that there would never be another singer like her.

CHARLIE PARKER

$\mathbf{P}$erhaps the single most influential figure in modern jazz, Charles Parker, Jr.,
was born in Kansas City, Kansas, on August 29, 1920.
His father, Charles, Sr., once a vaudeville performer,
worked as a railroad chef, spending long periods of
time away from home. Finally, when young Charlie

was eight, his father left for good. An only child, Charlie grew up under the influence of his mother, Addie, a strong and devoted woman who kept things together by working long hours cleaning other people's houses.

Addie Parker urged her son to work hard in school, and his good grades encouraged her to believe he might become a doctor. However, when he reached high school, Charlie discovered the alto saxophone. Mastering the instrument soon became the passion of his life.

Along with a few school friends, Charlie formed a band called the Deans of Swing and played at dances and parties. His musical activities soon affected his schoolwork; when he was left back a grade, he decided to drop out and devote himself to music. Before his musical career was fully under way, he became a married man. Just short of his 16th birthday, he wed his high school sweetheart, Rebecca Ruffin, and the newlyweds moved into Addie Parker's house.

An early turning point in Parker's life came shortly after his marriage, in 1936, when he took part in a jam session at Kansas City's Reno Club, a mecca for top-flight jazz musicians. Hoping to make an impression, Parker took a solo during one of the club's famous jam sessions and faltered badly. After being hooted off the stage by the veterans, he left the club with an angry determination to redeem himself. With the help of a friend, he spent months studying music theory, working out chords and harmonies over and over on his horn. Finally, he was ready to begin his career in earnest.

Unfortunately, at this time Parker also began to develop the personal problems that were to make so much of his life a misery. He had been exposed to marijuana and alcohol at an early age, and by the age of 17 he had taken up heroin. To the dismay of his wife and mother, he began to pawn household items to support his drug habit, and his moods would swing suddenly from happiness and charm to anger and menace. Not even the birth of a son, Francis Leon, was enough to stabilize his personal life.

His musical life, however, began to flourish. After a stint in Buster Smith's band and a brief stay in Chicago, Parker set out for New York City. But he had a difficult time finding work and had to take a job as a dishwasher in a Harlem night spot. He did, however, have a chance to hear some of the great jazz innovators, such as the pianist Art Tatum, and to sit in on jam sessions with practiced players. During one of these sessions, he hit upon a unique method of improvising chord changes and developed a style that would soon create a revolution in jazz.

Before that happened, Parker returned to Kansas City in 1939 for his father's funeral. While there, he accepted an offer to join the Jay McShann Orchestra as first saxophonist. Around this time he also acquired the nickname Yardbird—later shortened to Bird—supposedly because of his extreme fondness for chicken.

His work with the McShann group earned Parker the admiration of his fellow musicians. But audiences were not yet ready for Parker's innovative solos, which seemed coarse and unmusical when compared with the mellow swing music that was the rage throughout the 1930s. Nevertheless, he continued to tour with McShann until 1942, when he decided once again to seek his fortune in New York.

After some difficulty, Parker found a spot in the Earl Hines Orchestra, but his unruly personal life began to get in the way of his music. His heroin addiction was now out of control. In addition, he had divorced his first wife, Rebecca, married the dancer Geraldine Scott, and then split up with Scott only a year later. His frequent absences soon led to his dismissal from Hines's band. After a brief stint with Billy Eckstine's band in 1944, Parker decided to devote his energies to smaller groups, where his creativity could be unleashed.

Parker now found a home on New York's West 52nd Street, where jazz clubs crowded both sides of the block between Fifth and Sixth avenues. At a club named the Three Deuces, he teamed up with Dizzy Gillespie, Ray Brown, Bud Powell, and Max Roach. With Parker and Gillespie leading the way, the quintet pioneered the bebop revolution throughout 1944 and 1945. Spurning the conventions of swing, they improvised fast-paced, free-ranging variations on familiar tunes that left their audiences breathless.

After Gillespie moved on to form his own big band, Parker remained on 52nd Street to lead his own combo, commanding a growing corps of devoted fans. At the time, he also made a series of recordings with Gillespie that became jazz classics, among them "Ko Ko," "Billie's Bounce," and "Now's the Time." When the 52nd Street scene began to decline, Parker's group made a historic visit to Los Angeles, where they introduced bebop to West Coast audiences.

When the rest of the group returned to New York, Parker chose to remain in California. He found work, but his heroin addiction was worse than ever; he could not have survived without the help of a handful of devoted friends, such as the talented young trumpeter Miles Davis and the bassist Charles Mingus, who looked after Parker's business affairs and let him stay in their homes. Despite his personal woes, his art was reaching its peak; the recordings he made for Dial Records in the spring and summer of 1946 are among the classics of bebop. By the end of the year, however, Parker had suffered a nervous breakdown and was committed to Camarillo State Hospital.

The care he received at Camarillo restored Parker to mental and physical health. He emerged from the hospital in early 1947, cut some more recordings for Dial, and then went back to New York. There he found the bop revolution in full swing. As one of the new music's great practicioners, Parker enjoyed unprecedented popularity, steady employment both in clubs and in the recording studio, and a good income. He also found some tranquillity in a third marriage, to Doris Sydnor, though this relationship, like the first two, was not to last.

In 1949, Parker made his first trip to Europe and achieved a triumph at the Paris Jazz Festival. Back home he experimented with different forms, including a string orchestra and a Latin jazz band, though his best forum was still the small combo. Among the high points of this period in Parker's life were a new romantic attachment—with Chan Richardson—that would last the rest of his life, as well as the opening of the club Birdland, named in Parker's honor. There was no name in jazz that had more luster.

But by 1951, Parker's indulgence in heroin and alcohol had become even more excessive. Because of his association with known drug dealers, New York State revoked his cabaret card, making it impossible for him to perform in nightclubs, and he was forced to go out on the road to make a living. His music suffered greatly from the lack of a stable group, and the routine of travel began to wear him down. Even when his cabaret card was restored in 1953, he found it hard to regain his former income; when his daughter, Pree, died of a heart condition at the age of two, Parker bitterly blamed himself for not being able to afford better care for the child.

In 1954, at odds with his musical colleagues and seriously depressed, Parker attempted suicide. He recovered, but his continuing unhappiness caused him to leave his wife and live like a vagabond, often sleeping on the subways or in the street. On March 12, 1955, while trying to recuperate from an illness in a friend's apartment, Parker suffered a fatal heart attack. The doctor who examined Parker's ravaged body estimated his age at 53. In fact, he was barely 35. His life was brief and tormented, but the legacy of his genius still inspires fans and musicians alike.

❦ FURTHER READING ❦

Louis Armstrong

Armstrong, Louis. *Satchmo: My Life in New Orleans*. New York: Da Capo Press, 1986.

Collier, James Lincoln. *Louis Armstrong: An American Genius*. New York: Oxford University Press, 1983.

Tanenhaus, Sam. *Louis Armstrong*. New York: Chelsea House, 1989.

Count Basie

Dance, Stanley. *The World of Count Basie*. New York: Da Capo Press, 1980.

Kliment, Bud. *Count Basie*. New York: Chelsea House, 1992.

Morgun, Alun. *Count Basie*. New York: Hippocrene Books, 1984.

John Coltrane

Selfridge, John. *John Coltrane*. New York: Chelsea House, 1994.

Simpkins, C. O. *Coltrane*. Baltimore: Black Classic Press, 1989.

Thomas, J. C. *Chasin' the Trane*. New York: Da Capo Press, 1976.

Duke Ellington

Collier, James Lincoln. *Duke Ellington*. New York: Oxford University Press, 1987.

Ellington, Mercer. *Duke Ellington in Person*. Boston: Houghton Mifflin, 1978.

Frankl, Ron. *Duke Ellington*. New York: Chelsea House, 1988.

Ella Fitzgerald

Colin, Sid. *Ella: The Life and Times of Ella Fitzgerald*. London: Elm Tree Books, 1986.

Kliment, Bud. *Ella Fitzgerald*. New York: Chelsea House, 1988.

Dizzy Gillespie

Gentry, Tony. *Dizzy Gillespie*. New York: Chelsea House, 1991.

Gillespie, Dizzy, with Al Fraser. *To Be or Not to Bop*. New York: Doubleday, 1979.

Horricks, Raymond. *Dizzy Gillespie*. New York: Hippocrene Books, 1984.

Billie Holiday

Holiday, Billie, with William Dufty. *Lady Sings the Blues*. New York: Penguin Books, 1984.

Kliment, Bud. *Billie Holiday*. New York: Chelsea House, 1990.

White, John. *Billie Holiday: Her Life and Times*. New York: Universe, 1987.

Charlie Parker

Frankl, Ron. *Charlie Parker*. New York: Chelsea House, 1993.

Giddins, Gary. *Celebrating Bird: The Triumph of Charlie Parker*. New York: Morrow, 1987.

Priestley, Brian. *Charlie Parker*. New York: Hippocrene Books, 1984.

❧ INDEX ❧

❧ Picture Credits ❧

The Bettmann Archive: p. 47; Frank Driggs Collection: cover, pp. 5, 12, 19, 26, 33, 54;
UPI/Bettmann: p. 40.

RICHARD RENNERT has edited the nearly 100 volumes in Chelsea House's award-winning BLACK AMERICANS OF ACHIEVEMENT series, which tells the stories of black men and women who have helped shape the course of modern history. He is also the author of several sports biographies, including *Henry Aaron*, *Jesse Owens*, and *Jackie Robinson*. He is a graduate of Haverford College in Haverford, Pennsylvania.